THE EGYPTIANS

Roger Coote

Thomson Learning • New York

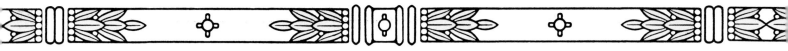

Look into the Past

The Aztecs
The Egyptians
The Greeks
The Romans
The Saxons
The Vikings

First published in the
United States in 1993 by
Thomson Learning
115 Fifth Avenue
New York, NY 10003

First published in 1993 by Wayland (Publishers) Ltd.

Cataloging-in-Publication Data applied for

ISBN 1-56847-061-4

Printed in Italy

Picture acknowledgments
The publishers wish to thank the following for providing the photographs in this book: Peter Clayton 16; E.T. Archive 7 (bottom, Cairo Museum), 22 (British Museum), 29 (both); Mary Evans 5 (bottom); Werner Forman 6 (Cairo Museum), 7 (top), 8 (Cairo Museum), 9 (left, McAlpine Collection), 13 (both, Cairo Museum), 14 (bottom, Egyptian Museum, Turin), 15 (bottom, left and right), 17 (bottom), 19 (bottom, Cairo Museum), 21 (top); Robert Harding Picture Library 9 (right), 17 (top), 19 (top), 21 (bottom), 24 (bottom); Michael Holford 11 (both, British Museum), 12 (British Museum), 14 (top, British Museum), 15 (top, British Museum), 18, 20 (British Museum), 23, 24 (top, British Museum), 27 (both, British Museum), 28 (British Museum); Wayland Picture Library 5 (top).
Map artwork on page 4 by Jenny Hughes. Artwork on page 10 by Stephen Wheele.

CONTENTS

Words that appear in **bold italic** in the text are explained in the glossary on page 30.

WHO WERE THE EGYPTIANS?

The *civilization* of ancient Egypt was one of the oldest in the world. It started about 5,000 years ago and lasted for more than 3,000 years. The ancient Egyptians were descended from hunters who lived in North Africa. Gradually they learned how to grow food by planting seeds and harvesting crops. At first, there were two separate kingdoms – Upper and Lower Egypt. Then, around 3100 B.C., these were united to form a single country ruled by a king, or pharaoh. When a pharaoh died, another member of his family became the new ruler. The pharaohs were divided into families called dynasties.

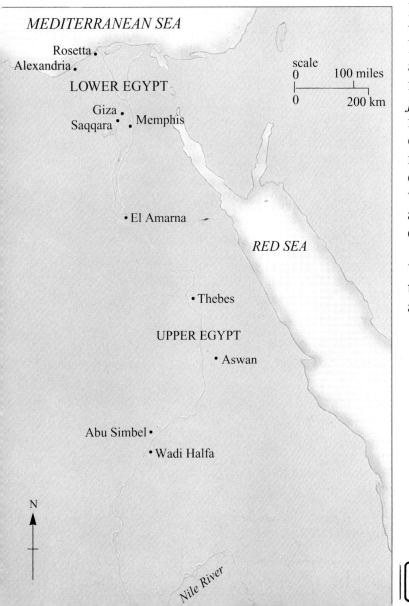

Egypt is a very hot, dry country and civilization was able to develop there only because of the Nile River. The river flooded each year, and after the floodwaters went down a layer of mud was left on the land. This mud was very *fertile* and it enabled the Egyptians to grow more food than they needed. This meant the extra food could be traded for goods that were not available in Egypt. It also meant that not everyone had to farm the land, so some people were free to work as architects, doctors, and artists, and to do other jobs that enriched the country's culture.

◄   This map shows most of the important towns and cities of ancient Egypt. They were all built along the Nile.

▲ Much is known about the Egyptians because ***archaeologists*** have found many remains of their civilization. Most of these remains are ***tombs*** in which dead people were buried. The Egyptians believed that people went on living after death, so great care was taken to bury the dead in pleasant surroundings with everything they'd need for daily life. Because of this, we have a good idea of what life in ancient Egypt was like. This tomb has been painted with scenes showing everyday life in ancient Egypt.

◀ The tombs in which pharaohs were buried contained the finest paintings, as well as beautiful jewelry, furniture, war chariots, and other valuable items. Most of these tombs were found by robbers who ***plundered*** them for their riches. But in 1922, an archaeologist named Howard Carter discovered a royal tomb, most of which had not been robbed. It belonged to Pharaoh Tutankhamen and it contained more than 2,000 separate objects, many of them priceless, and all of them clues to what life in ancient Egypt was like.

RULERS AND PEOPLE

The pharaoh was the supreme ruler of Egypt, although he gave some power to nobles and officials. The vizier was the chief minister and judge, and he controlled the government. Below him were the governors of the "nomes," the areas into which the country was divided. There were also officials of the royal court and magistrates who made sure that the laws were obeyed. The army was controlled by the pharaoh or his son, the crown prince. The *temples* were run by a powerful group of priests and priestesses.

◀ Egyptians regarded their pharaohs as gods. The pharaoh and his wife lived in great luxury and wore the finest clothes and the most expensive jewelry. This picture shows the back of the throne found in Tutankhamen's tomb. The throne was made of wood covered with sheets of gold and silver and decorated with colored glass and jewels. In this scene, Tutankhamen's queen is dabbing his collar with perfume.

After the pharaoh, the most powerful ▶ people in Egypt were nobles and senior officials, many of whom were close relatives of the pharaoh. This picture shows a nobleman and his wife. Most Egyptian men, not including the pharaoh, had just one wife. Although most Egyptian women did not have any political power, they did have freedom and independence. Men and women had equal rights, and married women could do what they wanted with their own money and possessions. A man who treated his wife badly might be taken to court by her family, or his wife could divorce him.

▲ Under the pharaoh and his officials and priests were the merchants and craftsmen, such as stonemasons, carpenters, and potters. Then came the farmers, fishermen, boat builders, laborers, servants, and, finally, slaves. In Egyptian law, poor people were treated in the same way as rich, and even slaves had some rights. Servants and slaves often helped to prepare and serve food. The two girls in this picture were servants in the house of a nobleman called Ti. The things they are carrying show the kind of crops and livestock produced on Ti's estates.

LANGUAGE AND WRITING

Some of our knowledge of the Egyptians comes from their writing. They carved or painted characters, known as hieroglyphs, on monuments, walls, and tombs. Hieroglyphs were also written on a type of paper called papyrus and on ostraca–pieces of stone and pottery. Written records were kept of business and legal matters. Most Egyptians could not read or write, however, and scribes were hired to do these tasks for them.

Hieroglyphs were letters in a type of picture writing called hieroglyphics, which consisted of more than 700 different **symbols**. Each symbol represented an object or a particular sound. Words were made of several symbols. This picture shows hieroglyphs that were carved and painted on the inside an official's coffin. The bird symbols are quails or chicks and can also stand for the English letter "w." The red oval symbols represent mouths and sound like the letter "r."

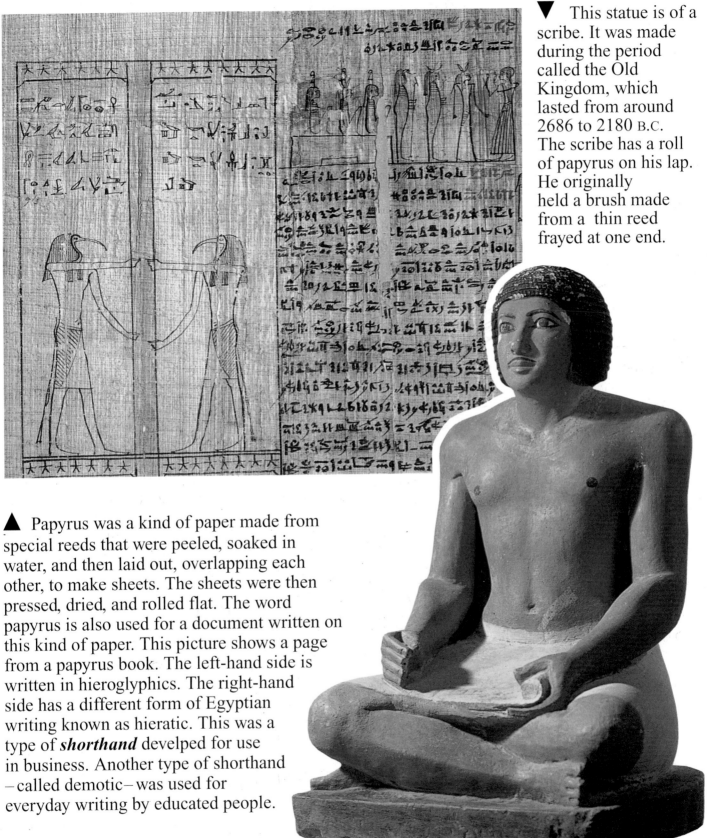

This statue is of a scribe. It was made during the period called the Old Kingdom, which lasted from around 2686 to 2180 B.C. The scribe has a roll of papyrus on his lap. He originally held a brush made from a thin reed frayed at one end.

▲ Papyrus was a kind of paper made from special reeds that were peeled, soaked in water, and then laid out, overlapping each other, to make sheets. The sheets were then pressed, dried, and rolled flat. The word papyrus is also used for a document written on this kind of paper. This picture shows a page from a papyrus book. The left-hand side is written in hieroglyphics. The right-hand side has a different form of Egyptian writing known as hieratic. This was a type of **shorthand** develped for use in business. Another type of shorthand – called demotic – was used for everyday writing by educated people.

HOUSES

The large temples and some of the palaces of the pharaohs were built with stone blocks by slaves and servants. The stone was *quarried* from cliffs and then dragged to the river on sledges. Boats then carried the stone to where it was needed. The houses where ordinary people lived, however, were constructed from mud bricks. These were made from mud that was baked in the hot sun until it was hard.

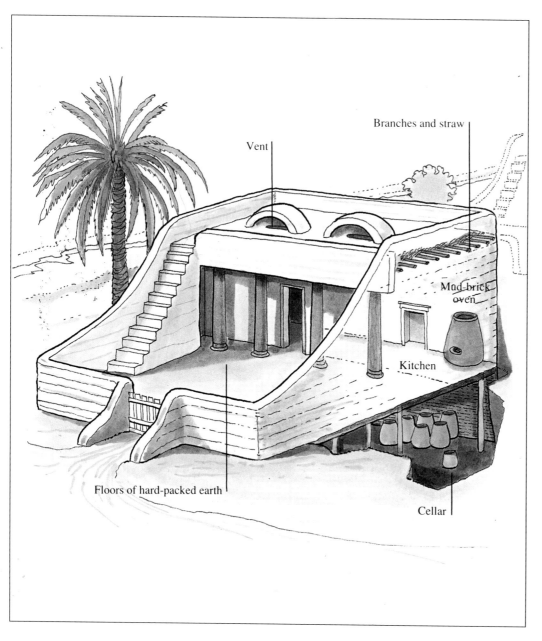

Branches and straw

Vent

Mud-brick oven

Kitchen

Floors of hard-packed earth

Cellar

This illustration shows a typical house built in about 1500 B.C. for a workman and his family. It was built of mud bricks and had a brick roof supported on palm tree logs. The roof above the larger rooms was held up by strong wooden columns. The walls of the most important rooms were plastered and sometimes decorated with *murals*. The house had only one story, with steps leading up to the roof.

▲ This papyrus from around 1300 B.C. shows a nobleman and his wife standing in their garden. They are making an offering to Osiris, the god of the dead. In front of the man is an ornamental garden pool and behind the couple is their house.

◀ This stone model is of a house built sometime after 1000 B.C. Like those of earlier times, these houses were made of mud bricks, but they had two stories instead of one. This made them tall and thin.

CLOTHES AND JEWELRY

For most of the year, the weather in Egypt was hot, so clothes were quite thin. They were made of linen, a fabric produced from the flax plant. Among wealthy Egyptians, fashions changed, but ordinary people wore much the same type of clothes throughout the whole period of Egyptian civilization. Men usually wore a short kilt and women wore an ankle-length tunic. In winter, when the weather was colder, people wore large cloaks made of wool.

This papyrus shows Hunefer, a wealthy Egyptian, and his wife Nasha. Both are wearing long linen tunics although Nasha's is of a finer material than her husband's. On her head, Nasha has a cone of perfumed wax. As the wax melted in the heat, it ran down the face and gave a pleasantly cool feeling. As with clothes, the hairstyles of rich people varied according to the period. Hunefer and Nasha have the elaborate hairstyles typical of their time, about 1310 B.C.

Many Egyptians wore jewelry, especially rings and earrings, but the rich also wore beautiful headdresses, *pectorals*, and bead collars. This necklace and pendant were found in the tomb of Tutankhamen. The pendant at the bottom is in the shape of a boat carrying a scarab beetle, which represented one of the Egyptians' gods. The disk above the beetle represents the sun. The scarab and sun symbols are repeated around the necklace.

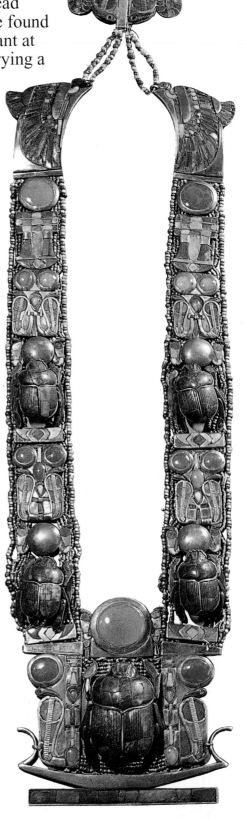

▲ Children wore their hair in a different way from adults. Young boys had their hair cut short or even shaved off except for one long lock on the side of the head. Young girls sometimes had a number of braids.

FARMING AND FOOD

Every July, the Nile River begins to flood. When the floodwaters go down in September, they leave behind a layer of fertile mud. Because of this flooding ancient Egyptian farmers were able to grow enough food to feed all the people and to trade with what was left over.

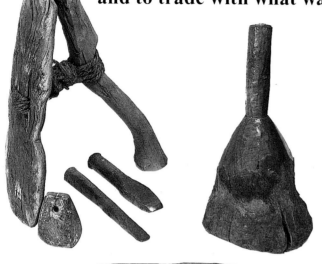

◀ After the floods had gone, farmers prepared their fields with plows made of wood and bronze. The surface of the soil was then broken up with rakes, like the one at the bottom of this picture. Then seeds were sown by hand and trodden into the ground by animals, which were driven across the fields. As the crops grew, weeds had to be dug out with a hoe, like the one on the left of the picture. (The other tools in the picture are a plumb bob, chisels, and a hammer, which would have been used by builders.)

▼ The most important crops grown in Egypt were wheat and barley. They were harvested in March and April. The grain was separated from the straw by being trampled by cattle. Then it was stored in a *granary*. The men in the picture are carrying grain up a ramp to the granary. Granaries were built above ground level to protect the precious crops from hungry rats and mice. The grain was used to make bread, which was the main food of poor people.

Farmers raised
livestock on the
hillsides near the Nile.
When the crops had
been harvested, herds
of sheep, cattle, goats,
and pigs were brought
down to graze on the
stubble that remained
in the fields. In this
scene, a herd of cattle
is being inspected.
Cattle were kept for
meat and milk, while
sheep provided
meat and wool for
warm winter clothing.
Only rich people
could afford to eat
meat.

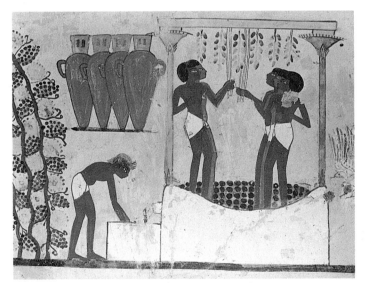

Sometimes the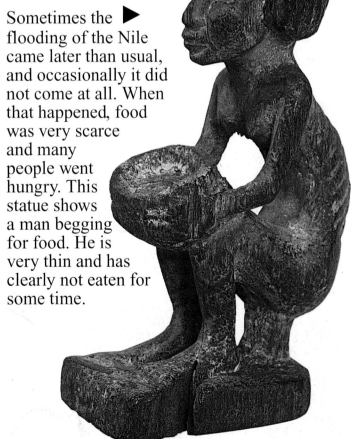
flooding of the Nile
came later than usual,
and occasionally it did
not come at all. When
that happened, food
was very scarce
and many
people went
hungry. This
statue shows
a man begging
for food. He is
very thin and has
clearly not eaten for
some time.

▲ Wheat and barley were not the only crops
grown. Vegetables, especially onions, were a
major part of most Egyptians' diet. Grapes
were also grown along the Nile. The men in
this picture are treading grapes to squeeze out
the juice to make wine. Ordinary people
mostly drank beer made from barley.

WORK

Because the land around the Nile was so fertile, not everyone had to work in the fields to produce enough food for the population of Egypt. This enabled people to do other kinds of work such as making pottery, building boats and royal tombs, carpentry, and engineering. There were even astronomers who used their knowledge of the sun and earth to create a solar calendar based on a 365-day year with twelve months. It is the basis for today's calendar.

Builders were very important in Egypt. The men in this tomb painting are making mud bricks, which were used for nearly all Egyptian buildings. The workers are mixing water with earth and straw. The mixture was poured into an oblong wooden mold. When the mixture had set, the brick was turned out of the mold and left in the sun to bake until it was hard.

▲ The craftsmen of Egypt were extremely skillful. They made beautiful jewelry, carvings, furniture, and other objects. This scene from a tomb painting at Thebes shows carpenters at work. They are making furniture, probably for a tomb or the home of a nobleman or other wealthy Egyptian. Some of the men are cutting wood with saws that look like those used today. The men at the top left of the picture are smoothing and polishing a piece of wood.

This picture shows metalworkers. The painting dates from about 1450 B.C. and was found in the tomb of the vizier Rekhmire, a famous law-giver, at Thebes. The craftsmen are making large copper vessels that were probably meant to be placed in the tomb with Rekhmire for him to use in the afterlife (see page 27). The man to the left in the picture is decorating a finished vessel by engraving a design on the surface. ▼

17

TRADE

Egypt was a great trading nation and traded with neighboring lands even before the country was made into one nation, around 3100 B.C. The main goods that were exported were *surplus* wheat, barley, linen, papyrus, and rope. In return, Egypt received gold, silver, copper, ivory, jewels, spices, ostrich eggs and feathers, *incense*, timber, and slaves. The Egyptians did not use money–instead goods were bartered, or exchanged, for each other.

▲ The Egyptians often used incense in their temple *rituals*. Because incense-bearing trees did not grow in Egypt, they had to be imported from the land of Punt (now called Somalia). The men in this picture are carrying incense trees to be loaded on to ships. The trees are being carried in baskets to protect their roots. After being unloaded in Egypt, the trees would be replanted.

Many of the countries with which Egypt traded could be reached overland, but it was often easier to use boats because they could carry more than pack animals, such as donkeys. This *relief* shows an ▶ Egyptian boat from between 2600 and 2200 B.C. It was probably a riverboat rather than a sea-going craft. All foreign trade was meant to be controlled by the pharaoh, but sometimes sailors secretly came ashore to sell their goods.

Ostrich feathers ▶ were used in ancient Egypt to make fans and decorative head-dresses. Although ostriches were found in Egypt and were hunted for their meat and feathers, extra supplies of feathers had to be imported from Nubia (part of the Sudan) to the south. This scene, from a small shrine discovered in Tutankhamen's tomb, shows Tuntakhamen and his wife. The headdress the queen is wearing is decorated with tall ostrich feathers.

LEISURE

There are many paintings and reliefs that show us how the Egyptians enjoyed themselves. Nobles held banquets where large quantities of food and drink were served to guests and entertainment was provided by dancers. Music and dancing were popular with both rich and poor people, as were board games. Children played with brightly colored leather balls, spinning tops, toy animals, and dolls.

This tomb painting, dating from 1400 B.C. shows musicians and dancers at a banquet. The girl in the center is playing pipes. Other instruments used included harps, lutes, drums, and tambourines. The Egyptians did not have a system for writing down their music, so we don't know exactly how it sounded.

Some dancers who were hired for banquets and other entertainments could also do acrobatics. This relief shows a group of acrobats turning somersaults. The relief was carved on the temple of Amon at El Karnak. The acrobats were performing for the crowds who would have gathered to celebrate a religious holiday.

This board game was found in Tutankhamen's tomb. It looks like a long, narrow chess board, but it is not known how the game was played.

21

One of the most popular pastimes among the rich was hunting. Animals such as gazelles, antelopes, stags, ostriches, and leopards were hunted with bows and arrows. In the marshes near the mouth of the Nile River, people hunted duck and other waterfowl. This painting shows a nobleman hunting fowl with his wife and daughter. The cat was used to frighten birds out of the reeds and then the hunter would attempt to bring them down by throwing a snake-shaped stick at them.

GODS AND RELIGION

The Egyptians worshiped many gods and goddesses, and each one could appear in a variety of forms. Temples were built for the gods where people believed they lived in the form of statues. Each day, the statue inside a temple was dressed and given offerings of food and drink. The pharaoh was thought to be related to Amon, the king of the gods.

This photograph shows part of the huge temple complex at El Karnak, on the eastern bank of the Nile River near Thebes. Built during the period known as the New Kingdom, which began around 1567 B.C. It is one of the largest religious structures ever built. It was designed to honor the most important god at that time, Amon-Ra, who was a combined form of two gods: Amon, the king of the gods, and Ra, the sun god.

23

▲ This papyrus from 1200 B.C. shows the god Ra in his boat. Like many other Egyptian gods, Ra was associated with a particular type of animal and was usually shown in the form of a man with a falcon's head. He was crowned with a disk representing the sun. Ra was often linked with other gods, including Amon, Sobek the crocodile god, and Horus the sky god.

◀ This painted relief from the Valley of the Kings shows Osiris, the god of the dead. He was the grandson of Ra and was married to Ra's sister, Isis, who was called the divine mother. Osiris and Isis were two of the most popular gods in Egypt and people believed that they had once ruled the country as king and queen.

DEATH AND THE AFTERLIFE

From the time of the Middle Kingdom (about 1991 to 1786 B.C.), it was believed that everyone went on living after death (before that time, only the pharoah was thought to have an afterlife). When a wealthy person died, the body was taken to the *embalmer*'s workshop. The embalmer took out the internal organs, including the brain and heart, and put them in special containers called *canopic jars*. The body was treated with special spices, oils, and perfumes and covered with salt to preserve it. It was then wrapped in linen. Seventy days later the funeral was held. During the ceremony, it was thought that the dead person's spirit crossed the River of Death and entered the Next World.

Anubis, the jackal god, was the god of embalming. Here we can see a priest, wearing an Anubis mask, embalming the body of a nobleman called Anhai. The picture is from a papyrus that was part of Anhai's Book of the Dead. Wealthy people were buried with their own Book of the Dead, which contained a map and various magic spells that would enable them to enter the Next World by passing through gates guarded by fierce serpents.

◄ When the body of a very important person ►
had been mummified (embalmed and wrapped
in linen), it was placed in a decorated mummy
case. This mummy and case belonged to a
priestess at Thebes, who died in about 1050
B.C. The case has been beautifully painted
inside and out. You can see mummies like this
in several museums around the world.

▼ Ordinary people were buried
in holes dug in the sand. Nobles
and pharaohs were buried
in special tombs. During the
Old Kingdom, pharaohs' tombs
were built in the form of huge
stone pyramids. Inside were
chambers containing the pharaoh's
mummified body and all of the
things he would need in the
afterlife. These pyramids at Giza,
outside Cairo, are some of the
most famous in Egypt. All of
Egypt's pyramids were broken
into by grave robbers. In the New Kingdom,
pharaohs were buried in tombs cut from the
rock at secret places in the Valley of the Kings.
Even so, most of these tombs were found and
robbed.

Even when Egyptians entered paradise there was work to be done in the fields. The figure in this picture is called an ushabti. Ushabti figures were buried with dead people and were supposed to do all the hard work in the Next World, leaving the dead free to enjoy themselves. ▼

▲ After entering the Next World, it was thought that the dead person was brought before a group of judges. He had to assure them that he had led a good life. Then the jackal god Anubis weighed the person's heart against the Feather of Truth while other important gods looked on. In the picture, the feather is on the right-hand side of the scales next to Anubis, and the dead person's heart is on the other side of the scales. The other gods are seated above the scales. If the heart was heavier than the feather, it meant the person had led a wicked life and would be eaten by a monster. If the heart was lighter, the person would enter a happy land and be greeted by all his dead relatives and friends.

27

WAR

Egypt was protected from most invaders by deserts and the sea. Even so, some attackers did get past these obstacles and the Egyptians had to fight to protect their country. Sometimes Egypt attacked neighboring countries, including Nubia, Syria, and Palestine. By conquering these lands, Egypt was able to obtain goods that it could not produce itself. For most of the period of ancient Egyptian civilization, all fighting was done on land. Ships were used for carrying troops and supplies but did not take part in battles until late in the New Kingdom.

Until about 1680 B.C. Egypt was not attacked by other countries. Then people known as the Hyksos invaded their land. At that time, the weapons used by Egyptian soldiers were slings, bows and arrows, spears, daggers, and axes. The Hyksos used curved swords, armor, and chariots pulled by horses. When the Egyptians managed to drive out the Hyksos they copied the weapons that had been used against them. This wall painting from the fourteenth century B.C. shows the Pharaoh Sethos I charging at his enemies in a two-wheeled war chariot.

This curved sword was another type of ▶
weapon copied from the Hyksos. Its handle
and sheath are decorated with jewels. Most of
the Egyptian army were infantrymen, or
footsoldiers. Although there were horse-
drawn chariots, there was no *cavalry*. The
pharaoh was the commander of the
army and he led his troops into battle.

▲ This picture shows part of a decorated
pavement from the Palace of Akhenaten at
Tell el-Amarna. It shows an archer carrying
his bow. Archers were used throughout
the history of ancient Egypt. There
were no guns in those days, and a
bow and arrow was just about
the only means of killing or
wounding an enemy at
long range.

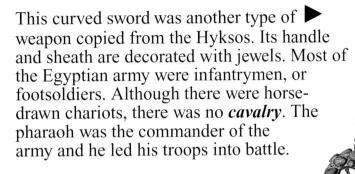

GLOSSARY

Archaeologists People who dig up and study objects from the past in order to learn about the civilizations that created them.

Canopic jars Vessels used for storing a dead person's internal organs to prevent them from decaying inside the body.

Cavalry Soldiers on horseback. The ancient Egyptians had no cavalry, but used horses to pull chariots instead.

Civilization A particular group of people and their way of life.

Embalmer A person who prepares dead bodies for burial.

Fertile A word describing land that is good for farming because it is rich in the nutrients that plants need to help them grow.

Granary A building in which grain is stored.

Incense A substance obtained from special trees, such as myrrh trees, which gives off a strong smell when burned. It is used during religious ceremonies.

Murals Large wall paintings.

Pectoral Large pieces of jewelry that were worn around the neck and hung across the chest.

Plunder To commit robbery or looting.

Quarried Dug or blasted out of the ground.

Relief A carving that is done on the face of a piece of stone.

Rituals Set ways of performing religious services.

Scribes People whose job was to read and write documents for others.

Shorthand A way of writing quickly, using abbreviations or symbols rather than whole words.

Symbol Something that stands for something else.

Surplus Leftover goods or supplies that a country can sell or trade.

Temples Buildings for the worship of goddesses and gods.

Tomb A structure built to contain the body of a dead person.

IMPORTANT DATES

Most of these dates are so old that historians argue over the exact years. All dates are B.C.

3100 Upper and Lower Egypt united into one kingdom.

3100-2686 The Early Dynastic Period.

2860 Papyrus is first used for writing.

2600 The first step pyramid built for Pharoah Djoser at Saqqarah.

2686-2181 The Old Kingdom (Dynasties III-VI) The Great Pyramid is built at Giza during Dynasty IV.

2325-2150 Trading at its height.

1991-1786 The Middle Kingdom (Dynasties XI and XII).
During Dynasty XI the Egyptian Empire grows, especially to the south. During Dynasty XII the arts flourish in Egypt.

1680-1568 Invasion of the Hyksos and their rule of Egypt.

1567-1085 The New Kingdom: Egyptian Empire at its largest.

1361-1352 Rule of Pharaoh Tutankhamen.

950-730 Dynasty XXII, when Egypt is ruled by Libyan kings.

664-332 The Late Period, when Egypt is ruled by Persian and Ethiopian kings as well as Egyptian pharaohs. Dynasties XXV-XXX.

332 Alexander the Great claims Egypt for Greece. Egypt is ruled by Greece and Macedonia until it becomes part of the Roman Empire in **30 B.C.**

BOOKS TO READ

Bendick, Jeanne. *Egyptian Tombs*. First Books. New York: Franklin Watts, 1989.

Giblin, James C. *The Riddle of the Rosetta Stone: Key to Ancient Egypt.* New York: HarperCollins, 1990.

Kerr, James. *Egyptian Farmers*. Beginning History. New York: Bookwright Press, 1991.

Oliphant, Margaret. *The Egyptian World*. New York: Franklin Watts, 1989.

Payne, Elizabeth. *The Pharaohs of Ancient Egypt*. New York: Random House, 1981.

Steel, Anne. *Egyptian Pyramids*. Beginning History. New York: Bookwright Press, 1990.

INDEX